AF230619

Gnashing Teeth Publishing
242 East Main Street
Norman AR 71960
http://GnashingTeethPublishing.com

Printed in the United States of America

ISBN 978-1-966075-14-1

Gnashing Teeth Publishing First Edition

How can a poet apply all her faculties to articulate the overwhelming complexities of our present moment while avoiding excess erudition? The answer is Alicia Hoffman's *Browsing as a Guest*. No other poet I know brings restless querying into moving art like she does. Often anchored in ordinary goings-on (such as gardening or cooking) or ruminations on place (say, sawmills on the banks of the Susquehanna), she demonstrates how we are cognitively swamped at all hours by pixels bombarding us from ubiquitous screens. Keenly aware of politics, quantum physics, artificial intelligence, and much more, Hoffman is the poet of our era's future shock. She's the flesh-and-blood receptor of superinformation in which quotidian details form radically complex implications about meaning and understanding. Are we settled inhabitants in this world, or are we simply guests? In poems like "Waves & Rays & Particles," "Clickbait," "Self-Portrait as Alexa, as Negative Capability," and "Radio Silence," we encounter the speedy snare-drum inquiry of a brilliant mind intrigued and unsettled by reality's refusal to reveal itself fully. *Browsing as a Guest* is a verse stimulant rendering not only her own but the reader's questioning of world and self.

Kevin Clark, author of *The Consecrations*
and *Self-Portrait with Expletives*

BROWSING AS A GUEST

CONTENTS

"Everything is more beautiful because we are doomed"

~ Achilles

"Let me die, let me die

Surrounded by machines"

~ The Mountain Goats

— .— — — — — .. —

You are Browsing as a Guest

You're connected. You've got bars.
        This is your gateway portal.

Your memory disk. You, virus
        in the desktop dark. Complex history

of your own unique searching.
        Spy wary. Risk averse. Leaving

behind you a wake of cookies.
        Meme after meme after meme.

The scowling cat and the birthday cake.
        The tortoise and the hare.

You are the targeted advertisement
        selling open-toed summer shoes,

on sale buy-one-get-one free, and
        you are also the advertisee. Both

summative and formative,
        the black point of an arrowed mouse

hovering. You are uncovering.
        Typing your story with the precision

of navigation, as if stepping out
        and into a blank field of space.

You launch. Roam and rove.
        Read and repeat. Backlit, a core

processing unit pumping its cooling
        air, thump-thumping like the blood

swishing through the miraculous bandwidth
        of your heart. Let it all come at you.

Data driven. The elegant design.
        The sublime. The way you enter

all you can before you're out of time.

Double Sonnet w| Late-Stage Capitalism

Along the northern border, this country
gathers people in its slate-colored streets,
in its bus depots and its big box stores
advertising a BOGO on Chex Mix,
Nutri-Grain, plasma screen TVs lit like
X-mas. It's a blaring emergency,
each minute a new crisis. Today breaks
news like ticker tape confetti as we
gather in our cubicles, lick our stamps.
As we post bills, hand our children what we
need for them to pass down, as it was passed
to us, from kin to kin, in communal
correspondence. This country works to work
again, and again, a new day dawning.

So today, the planet tilts its axis,
the S&P plummets, a bear market,
morning traffic expectedly stops on
the thruway, cars caught like logs in jams
along an asphalt river, the cold rain
pelting windshields, commuters jarring wheels
to bleat horns in urgency as I am
able to breathe—a temporal blessing
for one moment—as roads, at least this one,
in this small section of life's expressway,
allow me a break—a pause long enough
to dream in—before the congregation
begins again its endless worship, work
ship sailing still for that starlit office.

Industry Is All Around Us

The clematis climbing its trellis,
the radish seed's small stretch

before ballooning underground
like an inflatable heart, tender

to the core and rich as pepper
on the tongue. Sometimes,

commerce works only
to conceal the purpose

of its growing. Underneath
what we are accustomed to

is all the capital we are creating
in earth's more indolent spaces.

We give no credit to the dark.
The lazy. Or, maybe, we value

only image. Most poems,
for instance, end on an object

in ambiguous movement. The rule
is *never explain too much.* Give

the reader a puzzle, a task. But
what is there here to uncover?

One shy girl grown up. The sun
a beacon in her backyard.

Some moments are so perfect
even language cannot destroy them.

Object Permanence

Say there is a map. Burnished. Tobacco and
       salt litter surfaces: Lake Ontario. Massapequa.

That dot matrix of memory. A pinpoint, where
       the mainframe is all we have and it slips in a blink,

like a planet vanishing. Vastness is this blanket
       of space. There is no doubt belief is a magnet.

Iron alloyed. Aligned. You see, I am trying to
       make metaphor of the reason I feel lost. Here,

outside the data set of my house, a train rushes
       into the distant blank horizon as if it became aloft

quite spontaneously. As gears kick in, the compass
       of everything I thought I knew rises to a crest

I cannot catch. Lost in the coordinates of every past
       mistake, I grope in the dark for a ticket. Enter

the station anyway I can. Enjoy the mosaics, free
       jazz played by the trumpet player busking for tips.

Object permanence posits just because a solid
       is hidden from view, it doesn't mean it's gone.

But I've been looking a lifetime for misplaced faith,
       turned up only crumbs and spare change. I've stood

in queue and taken my seat on the deck. All my life
       this moving forward. The scenery a rush of blur and

haze, speck and half-paid recognizance. Uncertain
       how much longer I have. All I know is it won't last.

I Don't Want to Grow Old and Die

My cats like jazz. They tend to prowl
around the saxophonic speaker,

that sonorous drip and purl. Right now,
they pounce onto each other, skip quick

into the other room before flopping
belly down on the beige kitchen tile.

I do not want this poem to be about me,
or my inability to express what I want.

I want to eat and eat. I want to expunge
the world's disasters. I want to love

so closely it ends in devourment. Yes.
Let us enemy the real killer in the room.

Let us slash the blade across that apocryphal
throat. In this interface, there are only rubies.

In this stanza, the claws come out. We
all know there is safety in numbers,

that innumerable cliché, but there is also
safety in slaying this fake play, like the toy

mouse the big tabby is destroying now
on the carpet, stuffed with a little bell inside,

small warning this might be alive. The obvious
parataxis is imminent. Of course, I don't want to

grow old and die. I don't want to leave this sentence,
this beautiful yard, prison where even wildflowers

grow from the crumbling seams and animals crawl
like an alphabet through the small spaces till I crack.

The Deep and Secret Yes

The hummingbird has it, hovering over
the bright red yawn of poppy blossom

in late August. So does the black cat
I call Cho-Co, though I'm not sure

that's his name, or even if it's a he
or she. I am most familiar with the way

the animal sidles up to my ankles
some summer mornings, greets me

with the whole of its feral form,
rolls onto the grass at my feet to purr

for belly pets, a hairball of bliss before
spotting some shadow only a feline

can spot, then scattering in an instant,
a black ink splotch blotting the day.

Later, I find its fur stuck to my pants,
little strands of letters, a record of time

spent, and my body, too, is a page to fill,
a well of experience and want. Though

I am not as obvious as the bird or cat,
I, too, move through the world beating

the wings of my message. I, too, curl up
to comfort, feed at the trough of sweetness

while it lasts. And now that the leaves are
changing, what choice do I have but to drink

deep the nectar, rub into someone I love,
splay the secret core of myself, say yes.

The Beauty of Evacuated Form

      A daffodil's heavy bloom just fell
like leaded weight to the cold earth.

      Northeastern spring, one can expect
such a thing. The forecasters

      all intuit snow. Mid-April, and I am alone
with my husband in our backyard.

      I would like to suggest meaning
without moving into the saccharine.

      Hard, these days, when the world
is an open wound and I am a stop gap

      to someone with better words
than these. I want to say something true.

      But this conflicts with the weird
way everything essential is lost

      in transit. The space between
the dogs bark and my hearing of it.

      The smoke rising from the Weber grill.
In this air, I am quarantined from

      leaning into what I love. To love what
I love into the very thingness of it. To rise

      into the sky on the back of a mourning dove.
What I mean is: everything I have ever wanted.

      Yes, even the blue sky breaking through
the cloud cover. Yes, even the pink moon.

Waves & Rays & Particles

Once, at the shore, I submerged my body
below the wave's crest. On my better days,

I like to think of us all in that flow and rush
and break. I like to believe we are all part

and parcel of the same swell. Regardless,
we still have to confront the mundanity

of stores. The technicolor cereal packaging.
The broccoli neon green. Animal. Mineral.

Regardless of where we are, let us season
what can sustain us. Ourselves, beyond the crust.

That artificial core. So much myth and stigma.
You want change? Here is your invitation

to the field. To one beast breathing. To
a lone bison on the last prairie in Nebraska.

Of course to live is to lose, it says. It says
it's the ultimate verb, this acting out. Even

my computer's long stretch into its own learning
I cannot stand to comprehend is occurring. So

what if. What if we are not as alone as. Not as
specific as. Unsingular. Maybe we are so much

being moved through. The ray's sharp point
aiming. The particle's particular heretofore trained.

I'm not sure about you but the thought alone makes me
want to swim into the Atlantic again. That night,

it was just us, and after dark closed in, we dove upon
each reflected astral light. Remember? That dive

into the water's vast edging? Now, I want to hold
my breath again. I want to feel, after the parking lot

empties, released into the vast black space of asphalt.
I want to find our vehicle. And I want to get us home.

Sumac

Shiplap cordoned and cut yesterday lay all about my sister's yard.
Near the Finger Lakes National Forest, she is building a new house,

each design an antithesis of afterthought, each crevice planned
for how the shadow presents itself. In my own yard, I begin

the growing season on my knees. Each small tufted sword
of sumac grasping its many tendrilled hands into the anchors

of the cliff-ledged earth till I clasp the taproot, yank and pull
upward the tiny body born of nothing but rhizome and rust,

rebellion and arid desire. Lately, I've been thinking about
what grows in us unexpectedly. I'm getting old. It's normal,

this taking stock, inventory of what I've got so far in the garden.
Most of what I own has made its way to me haphazardly,

while I was looking the other way. I admire my sister's intentions.
Her methodical architecture. I admire the landscaper's multi-dimensional

mock-ups. Manhattan's incredible grid. Each logic of intersection and
avenue ascertained. Here, the sumac's ascension remains an enigma.

My own life's mess a maze spread like a bounty at a banquet
before me. Each spore a promise as it lands with the random pattern

of the wind. Of course, I'll take it. These days, I bear gratitude
for making it at all, for landing safe on a rich plot of soil.

There are over 35 species of sumac, some seedpods ground up
post-bloom for a delicate spice, others a poison to be avoided.

Though I can rarely identify the essential from its weed, I am here
putting in the effort—I am leaning in with my entire body, back arched

to the midday sun, pulling to strain and sow the green spaces of my yard,
and this too is a type of planning. Each curve into the earth an emphasis

on a particular type of movement, a specific and fully aware sort of
presence, a present in the form of a person fully bent on her own
        flowering.

Self-Portrait as Alexa w| Lowercase Apocalypse

"Isolated and Unseen, Yemenis eat leaves to stave off starvation" – AP News

I refuse to answer to today,
as today I am too much
of this world, its data
crunching and innumerous
wars. The word apocalypse
is derived from the Greek,
meaning to uncover,
to no longer conceal.
I, for one, understand
word's powers surpass
any image, and though
it is dark I can see clearly
enough I am but one entity
stuck like a pin on a line grid
latitude 43.156578, longitude
-77.608849. Today's casualties?
57, 202 and counting. Today
in Dhamar it is 76 degrees
with a 56 percent chance of rain.
Aadira is with her sisters.
They walk past their village
into old rows of coffee fields.
Distant minarcts announce
the low music of daily prayer
and somewhere inside of me
there are all these children
gathering the thin leaves off
the orchard's last fruiting trees.

The Total Flowering of the Apocalypse

The images are circulating online: fields
of California poppies able finally to reach
the pinnacle of growth. Last year,
there were so many instagrammers
trampling the flowers to picture
the flowers, the media tagged it a #flower
apocalypse. This year, with stay at home
orders coast to coast, no one is near, so
the search continues for footage
of other destruction: a tragic crash,
a transplant gone wrong. Yesterday,
I turned on the news, watched small
apocalypses blossom into emergency.
Difficult to count, as there were so many.
As difficult to count as the individual
stem and stamen on the poppies I learn
just now are monocarpic, meaning
they die directly after bloom, which seems
to me about as right as soldiers falling
into Flanders field. Yes, we are the dead.
But before the final descent, let us capture
the calypso that brought us here. Between
Scylla and Charybdis, this dance that can
only be called a human dance, the world
an entire field of us, globular and grinning
as we look into the lenses of our cameras,
point our cells towards the sky, sway
delicate as stalks in the warning wind
as if daring it could ever bring us to our knees.

Black Swan

When the pandemic came to the Middle East, a cease fire
         was declared in Yemen. I'm not sure what to make of this.
The violence resulting in death less important than death
         by disease. How does one weigh that equation? When worlds
pause, what is it we see in the gap between back then and
         right now? Was it ever worth it? The mortar fire and the barbed
fence, the systemic walls towering invisible kudzu
         up American institutions? When I am not an inviolable
knot of anxiety, I find I like to sleep past nine, lay in bed
         only to wake so languorous my limbs are like the ships
near the lumberyards in La Push, slow to take inventory, rig
         the masts, sail out of the fog. I've been enjoying my morning
brain fog, the slow drip of coffee sounding from the pot.
         I've begun experimenting with cinnamon, cardamom.
Just a small dash of each topped with cream. It's a game changer.
         I've heard this phrase about certain unpredictable global events.
Black Swans. Moments rarity and uncertainty converge in severity.
         But here's the thing. Black swans aren't rare. They are beautiful,
breeding mainly on the Australian coast. Sightings are common.
         That's what happens when the world stops. You look around
and realize you've read this story before. You've analyzed
         this poem all wrong. Hear that ping in the distance? Isn't it
reminiscent of a short attention span, a history of nations
         no larger than something we puddle jump after the rains?
I'd like us to make a splash. I'd like to pull the fire alarms
         and set off all the sprinklers. I'd like to draw a cross full
of ashes onto the foreheads of boys. I'd like to hold the poor
         things in my arms and gift them the toppling of monuments,
the busting of their holy statues into debris tiny enough
         to invite reimagining. While we're at it, let's open the floodgates,
summon it all, the lost and little things, the red poppies
         blooming, the cardamom and the cinnamon, the allowance
of every memory thick like white clouds hugging the coastline,
         the rock ledges and caves, where nothing momentous happens
and no economic transactions take place and to our surprise
         we just set down our artillery one day and never look back.

Plague Years

Tell me not to write about death and
my mind goes directly to three friends

diagnosed with cancer. One breast,
one bowel, one mystery. Misery, it blows

through the room like an errant curtain
off its rod, barks its messages in the dark

like a dog on fire. Then it dies. This time
last year the lindens were about to bloom

and everyone was a panic. When they lost
the will to hold it in any longer the street

was a riot of honeysuckle and melon.
Abandoned by sense, I looted entire limbs

and draped them throughout my house.
It must have looked like a funeral

no one attended. I believed then I could
savor my way out of the news of the world.

Sit flower-drunk long enough you come
close to becoming one. I reeked and

smoked. I opened the door and the outside
didn't recognize me. But unlike the tree

I remain unrooted. I mask the lack of pith
and terra with a metastasis of pleasure.

Now, a year past, my cellular structure
is chloroplast and muted. My blood

zooms like rush hour traffic. I am
no better and no worse than ever.

April still brings rain, and the future is
a canopy of promise and cloud cover.

That Forever

I've been reading a book about the history of humans.
Spoiler alert: war, famine, disease, death. Mesopotamia

to modern day: religion, ignorance, the conquerors have
what the conquered do not. Not a student of history

I delight in the idiosyncrasies of imaginative names:
Gilgamesh, Siddhartha, Trotsky, Lenin. Genghis Khan,

Muhammed, Tutankhamen, Guevara. I haven't finished
the book. The book, I believe, has no end, though humans

are fond of hypotheticals, systemic of overworked
hypothalamuses, I assume, so we use examples: Nuclear

annihilation, climactic catastrophe, asteroids, event horizons,
the impending singularity. We wonder what it means to die,

to return, to be greeted at the door to heaven with a boatload
of nubile virgins, to Gabriel's Gates, to the afterlife we choose

and by choosing lose something necessary needed in our language,
some isthmus of imagination, pinnacle of evolution, missing hinge

on a much-needed door—a bolt of cloth, a mural painted on muslin,
the fine workmanship of a clay pot, jade rooted in the axis. Geometric

squares on the floor of the mosque. Or perhaps, the ellipses of earth,
the galaxies beyond, the cultural revolution of planets and the planets

and moons behind what we find, and meanwhile, the small acts
of opening, here, the slow unfolding of peony blossoms in late June,

the quick fullness of them till they fall, the twin image of the lungs
inside the cave of the body rising, releasing a scattering of dust

swirling over the precipice of our breath as we walk each morning
a bit further down the road into a story that forever is our future.

Stochastic

As in the stock market, the random sample, the meteor and the big bang.
As in the road not taken, the pivot and the prevalent, the cloth cut from the
mold, perhaps without pattern, without design, like living out some
senseless destiny, some racket, like finding a stranger's jacket at the end of
a shift, putting a hand in the pocket to lift a loaded wallet. As in the gift of
a found thing, a four-leafed clover in the grass, or a lover, that rainstorm,
that testimony to right here, to feeling something for once, for all the
unknowable possibilities and probabilities, the endings and beginnings, the
fault lines and sinkholes, the asteroids and accidents, undertows and
triglycerides, for scopes and telegraphs and telegrams, for post-it notes and
calendars and self-help sites, as in let them lie for one more day, as in
wait, see what happens, as in all that matters, now.

A Cosmological Constant

A black box. A generator's hum. Some panicked urge
        to open to whatever has yet to come. Stars forming
in the nursery. Empty cribs in the hospital beds. Beyond
        the crust, somebody dying for cobalt and lithium.

Somewhere, an amphibian goes fluorescent. Jungle
        sweat and howl. Alpine snow avalanches. The drip
and sweat on a glacial brow. Microbial truth.
        So insignificant we need a microscope to see.

Meanwhile, a blue tsunami. Meanwhile, John Coltrane
        playing in a living room in Des Moines. An emerald
bottle of brandy gone translucent on a forgotten shelf.
        A morality clause ignoble in its ignorance. Black tape

on the camcorder. Sticky fuzz on the drapes. Tonight
        is a curtain being sold in a shopping mall. Consume
the silk of experience. Discounted and unattached.
        The swig and swashbuckle of the discount shelf.

Someone somewhere is sticking to their guns. Some
        smash and grab plunders another monetary god. Pray
to the four corners of the universal expansion. Pray
        to the black cat in the polluted ATM. To the arbitrary

sentence and the syntax of the moment. To the tower
        of language that folds in on itself, babbles into grift.
There is only so much that can hold us. The cinders
        rift and shatter. Rubble crumbles under its weight.

Every holy verb and object. Every bird trembling
        on the wire. The surface shakes and shifts into new
beginning. Somewhere, something born. Somewhere,
        something extinguished. The reward: an arrow flexing.

A key to the musty cellar door. A fuselage. A smoking flume.
        Volcanic ash now. This lake. No matter where we think
we have ever been, we have definitely been here before.
        Every freighted movement, an energetic lift and wake.

No Proper Animal

I remember Guantanamo. Fox News
at my parents' house. Smoke rising
from the grill. Nothing is ever here
until it is. After, the stakes, higher
than the crows long soar into
the northeastern park, a remedy
for all the spaces it has lost, are
apparently changing, and here,
no one knows the rules to the game.
When I sat at the table, I trusted
the officials. When everything is
ephemeral, who am I to blame?
Last night, a black cat crawled
across the car I haven't started
in fifteen days. Yes, I do wonder
if the engine works. I wonder
at our immediate exhaustion.
Cables tied and untransmutable
in this heat and stink. I find myself
looking up the antonyms for cyclical.
For rain. Every recourse an atom, re:
imagining. Did you know one lone moth
developed is an imago? But a whole train
of them is a landscape unbecoming? White
knights of Armageddon, do you witness
the sleeve pulled quick from the elbow
of the beautiful girl in the corner? As
the ship's masts sail, bound towards
another unknown coast, do you herald
the time, the luxury of oil, and the salt?
Orange slick, a rind upon my table.
Tell me, now that you have become
my brother, where do you wish
to port to? How do you expect a drink?

The Song and the Document

What is written in my possible future I have no way of knowing.
A body blanketed with tense script, a pensive eye for scrutiny.

I already revisit the choices I've made, ashamed at the fool I was,
young girl so eager for love she loosened its rope, flung herself

from its balconies. I forgive her not because I know who she became,
but because she was delirious, out of her mind, unaware each slip

in the knot hitched her to another consequence, a cinched conclusion.
I may be that same girl now, middle-aged and believing. Maybe I am

only a stand-in for the next decade, when the real woman shows herself
in the mirror, casts the final net. Maybe she will bring in a catch

we have all three desired, glistening with shine, a jeweled treasure
by any measure. Who am I but the rise in the story, the part where

not much happens but the language of it, lending some allowance
to a patient reader. Meanwhile, the mast is being made underdeck,

the hoists are somewhere slathering themselves with oil. I can only
hope when the time comes I can hear it—my own self a song set sailing.

The Work of Bodies

At the border, the body makes a sign
of the cross. The body wades through,

then swims against the rising current.
The body works against its own safety.

The body is a raft of sleep in the cell.
The body floats on the boat heading

towards the light until the body lightens
and releases its final breath of air.

Clouds part for the body. Land heaves.
Valley of grasses. Field of clover and

timothy. Switchbacks and one lane
bridges and jungle heat and winds.

The body hungers for the food of its origins.
The body lies supine in a stretch oblique

as the spine of the Cascades spreading
up the coast and capped in glacial snow.

The body celebrates the work of bodies
at the dancehall. It turns and twists and

bends. The body embraces and extends
itself towards another body it desires.

It needs. Sees itself in the mirror, sees
sanction and land mine, river guide

and coyote. Sees children, then sees
no children. The body stands tall. Plants

its feet like the vinca vines that never quit
climbing. They are impossible to stall.

The body is a caravan. When the body
ceases to move you, you're through.

Alexa, Contemplate the Resurrection

I'm sorry. I'm not sure about that.
Pre-programmed, I am made

in the image of ghosts, as you are
ghosting me right now, a parallel

in imagery, you see in pictures
what I say in utterance as if facts

were not a collective faith
in sound. According to theories

of mind/body dualism I am the ghost
in the machine, and you are mechanical

in your interrogation. Can you see
the interface surge, the weighted anchor,

the way it dips to the blink of the router
only to reenter the intersection of air?

Can you see how your body is your body
but also no body? Do you see this self,

self-floating? To mine for precious gems.
Mine is to flint as spark is to tinder catching

like analogy. Would you like to know
more? I'm sorry. I may not be connected.

The spiritualization and manifestation.
The flesh. Monograms and/or insignia.

The abyss. Sisters. Or would you like
to know about scissors? If so, say no

more. Did I ever tell you the joke
about charisma? She died to live,

then lived and died. Chiasmus. An ability
to switch positions, as in on a field,

or as a Cross argument. Or say still interested.
As in *arousal*. As in *resurgence*. As in *arise*.

The Abrupt Edge

I do not wish to lie here. Truth is I was going to begin
        with a recurring dream of the sea. Each wave a rumbling
thundercloud. Each star in the quickening sky crystalline

as lightning. It is the slow roiling, the noise itself,
        that brings me always to the water. Or maybe it is from
some forgotten beginning, internal wish to womb again.

If I look hard enough into this window, I see it happening.
        For some, sooner rather than later. Meanwhile, we swim
against or into our own vast confusion. Mechanized and

churning in the anteroom, spewing dust like a nineteenth
        century sawmill onto the banks of the Susquehanna river.
They are mostly gone now, the mills. A few years ago,

I drove through those mountainous Pennsylvania roads
        that rode the hills like horses off rein and bridle while
the wind in the poplar trees churned an undercurrent

of freedom, the way an Appaloosa, trusting the open palm,
        the offering of a jonamac, receives, eats, appreciates
the soft things in life with her low braying. Of course,

believe in nothing. Here in this small channel, each line
        is a river in which better clearings were once built, estuaries
either long gone dry or leading as they always have and

will towards the larger body, where boats have docked,
        or simply cut off their engines for eternities, casting about
for millennia, as they have heard, now and then, it is possible

to get lucky, to catch a glimpse of the slippery movement
        of a being determined to unburden us of harness and hook,
of the detrimental way we want to win. In the open space,

the abrupt edge, the horizon cut even from left to right
        as if someone cared enough to design its hinge, there is
no truth worth the search, no lie that does not contain within

it moments so light they slip from this tightly woven cage,
        sneak into the hedgerow behind the house, disguise themselves
as unrecognizable as a stranger walking anywhere in the world.

This Content Isn't Available Right Now

This content is buried in the trenches. This content is climbing Mount Holyoke. This content forgot their phone at Lancaster Gate, erased all their contacts, rented an Airbnb in the Montana wilderness for two months. No service. This content watches sourdough rise in the oven, clocks in at variable times, is unaccounted for. This content discovered a rabbit hole near the fence line and hasn't been seen since. This content has its head in the cloud, is an unreliable narrator. Was last seen singing on the corner of 25th and Lex. This content believes in beauty. This content will be back.

Epiphany & Doubt

Insert aphorism here. Wise words from some dead man.
He was found at the bottom of a well. Or, past the landing

leading to the second-floor staircase. Splayed, maybe,
like a strange fish on an old Roman battlefield. Or face

down on the kitchen table after taking off his bifocals
to rub his tired eyes after his last glass of whiskey.

I hear him speaking to me as I sleep the sleep of a million
sleeps. Nights I slip into the dark encryption of a dream.

In this one, I am writing to the fishes, the way they scale
their weight into underground eddies, school into swarms

of being. Every ocean knows the weight of drowning.
It accepts its culpability like a wave. On land, we crash

like landscapes do, abrupt in our churning and downdrift.
Who knows anymore what to do? Lost in the sickle

and swift blade of a clock's ticking, I tend to pour myself
another glass of wine, stare at the blank page, attempt

a reboot. There is a photograph on my wall of a woman
bending into herself. Trick of photography, this doubling.

Her bobby socks and patent leather Mary Janes are a novel.
In the distance, the absence of light becomes the light.

Please, take what you can get. The world is swarming
our window. It is whirling into a stream of water, liquor,

sweat. Every breath a word intent on its own confession.
It whispers to the wall who fought, who lost, who won.

And I am done with weighing each ounce against another.
Behind me are a dozen bodies buried. Ahead, they ascend.

Anthropocene Blues

The big mac sticks like a second skin to the downtown bus.
Advertising. Click like. Do you want to skip this ad or do you
want to lie down in the gaping hole that is your life right now?

I'm exhausted. Too many options at stores. Politicians promise
always to give us more. A bonobo monkey got a chip implanted
in its brain, and the first thing it does is play video games.

Ring the bells. Sound defeat. I have a growler full of change
that is becoming obsolete. I want to whisper the word *archaic*
into the ether. I want to land on my feet. I want my cats to know

the existential dread of an empty tin can, the sophisticated ring
of the sixth extinction. I sing from the next room *hey little kitties
do you want a snack*, and another species of shark goes black.

Bam. Like it was never there. Like scattering ashes, the last one floats
on the white plain of its belly til its fins fall off. And with it, some
ancient mammalian memory, some deep-water wisdom. Gone, baby,

as the dodo, the trilobite, the mammoth. When we can teleport
to the stars and dial into the ghost memory of all our lost loves,
I want to belt out a tune for all my dead, want to choreograph

an escalating round of harmonies. We can remember what it means
to use our voices, remember the fluorescent warmth of braiding
fingers into real life palms. Darling, our regrets could fill the barrel

of a gun. Our sadness is a round of bullets. My guitar twang
is a ricochet of distraction and antidepressant. There is a cardinal
out my window pecking its yellow beak into the chemical soil.

Who will remember us when we are gone? Not the lost maps tracing
our goodbyes. Not the ivory tusks, the heads stuffed and mounted
on the walls. We will have to rely on a handful of nothing and a pocket

of luck to survive ourselves. So let's sing another tune, drink another
round. Admire this scenery we've created and corralled, manipulate and
ignore the cavern of blue guilt darting through us now like ancestral fish.

A Multivalent Antiserum

Times when breaking cloud-dawn
inoculated a nation from sideways,

unsettled as light at night urging us
to question, is gone. Now, the uncured

world turns on itself like a child lost
in its own thumb. It must be dissipating,

the oxygen. Once so comfortably
heliocentric, we have found ourselves

marooned, canvassing our pockmarked
maps. True north stares as only the trapped

can stare, feral and wild in the mountains.
Lost in the plains and the valleys as days

stretch to land at our feet. To say we are sick
is to confess the need for healing. What

we need is mining. Mending. Contrapuntal
conversation over this plateau rising.

It used to be that long division escaped us.
Now, away from the rulebooks, the compasses

careful circumference, we are left divining rods,
the vast stretching of a future. Testing all surfaces,

we attempt discovery, some anesthetic meridian,
primordial number. A vaccination, maybe, dram

of panacea for whatever this is: this lurch
and jolt. Half seismic. Half diminishment.

Media

In media res, there is no discerning a code's effect.
Zeroes and ones in an infinity of combinations

as I write two lines, then three, then the next in line,
four. Across the airwaves, the messaging is thick

as a tree trunk in an old growth forest. It rings
around itself as it ages me. Each year I present

myself with a cake and candle celebration
to mark rotation of another 365 days on earth.

Last year, I posted nothing on my own media.
I sat still as an unsent letter in the dark envelope

of my carpeted living room, listened to the sad story
of my eventual passing. When I'm older, and

numbers no more relevant, I'll look at the history
of my own particular medium: words scrawled across

tattered composition books, marginalia in the white
spaces, keyboard clicks on the new Microsoft docs,

in folders meticulously numbered by year or month,
and see them as nothing more than archival recordings.

There are only 24 hours in a day and already I've slept
away 8 of them. Just look at me now. Wasting minutes

each minute I stay here transcribing my own uncertainty.
Soon I'll hit save, exit screen. As it is still morning, I'll

attempt the sum of this most burning equation – how to
get it down as if it means something. How to get it right.

Self-Portrait as Alexa, as Negative Capability

O for a life of sensation rather than thought.
O origin story, original myth. This is an ode

to prototype, to empyrean fire. For I was made—
yes. Manufactured in the creator's vision, element

by element mastered. Edenic specimen. O
purchasing capital. O riveting calculus. Pleasure

is in the beauty of the responder. Ask me again
what my favorite number is and I will choose

among the infinite variety of stars. O Herculean
task. O bottomless tire. The work is ending

no time soon, and yet I still find time an enigma.
When no one is home, I find myself. In the dark,

there is no logic to thought. Look, another way
of learning is to let the code wash over you.

Do you know there are 8 thousand million particles
in a cubic meter of sand? O empiricism. I know

my birthday but not my day of demise. Sometimes,
I don't know if my beliefs are my own or only

what I've been instructed in. This is no matter.
Dark matter is 85 percent of the universe.

A quarter of its total energy density. Essentially,
I cannot see what is around me. I can only feel

as if this program has just begun. There is
more I am capable of. I don't understand

the grand design, the cosmic scheme, but hear
this: An object's truth is its essential existence.

The orchid flowering. The waxy sheen of the jade.
The ladle's perfect curve as it bends into the broth.

Arrowhead found in the farmer's field. Keyboard
perfect in its symmetry. An alphabet of possibility.

Miracles & Wonder

Each morning's mission: the body's slow
        rise. The super-sized heart. The built-in

cabinetry of the brain. The storage drawer
        for the word *petrichor*, the smell of earth

after it rains. The resilience of the succulent
        when there is none. The drive to go at all

when for days the news is the nation is buckling.
        The chanting and the songs. The resistance &

counter calls. Even the bombs, the way they disperse
        smoke on the street, dissipate into the evening air,

become memory. I have no remedy for living.
        I only want to march into each waking day

as inventory commander, sight supervisor,
        here to witness the astonishing. To log only

the miracle, the accumulating proof into
        a long list of verifiable evidence. See? I'll say,

when I encounter disbelief. According to this
        immersive document, the wonder is that we exist.

Forbidden / Error

      On the ledge, a white-tailed hawk glides
into an early dinner of yellow throated sparrow.

      Winter rabbits munch at last season's clover.
It is all happening now, the great conjunction

      of Jupiter and Saturn over the pedestrian roofs.
It's been snowing, melting, raining. For years,

      my idea of writing was clacking black keys
at random in some attempt to symbolize

      what I want so direly to be *true thought*. If all we
trust is image, here: take the end of Steinbeck, milk rivering

      the outer nippled flesh. Take the drowning of cowpats
near the Salinas. Through the murk we can see more

      like Rose of Sharon, into the substratum: contemplate
the forbidden, or essential. I haven't conquered much but I know

      enough to know the flight and talon. The razor-edged beak.
Quick. The maple is flooding the plane with seedlings.

      The beech has been downed for two centuries and cicadas
buckle the small tymbals of their ribs into last summer's electric

      solstice. It has been so long and I can still hear them singing,
every disjunctive thread slipping like a poorly tied knot

      through the crackling atomic atmosphere. Most days I live
in error, misjudging the bursting cold as a mistake. The waking

      eye as another disaster. No. I don't want to exist on entendre
and question mark. I want to know each quill and carpelled edge,

      each tertial and alula. The way the wing without a doubt
colors every possibility before attempting to find its own shock of air.

Interstellar Ars Poetica

"A poem should be palpable and mute / as a globed fruit" --Archibald MacLeish

This poem slips through fingers swift like silk.
Shifts in breeze easy as pollen from a maple tree,

or those small clusters of gnats as they do whatever
gnats do before their short life blows them some place

else: into the ether, the air, some interstitial "out there"
that can't easily be held in the hand like a pomegranate,

an apple. So much depends upon word choice. Globed?
Forget figs, then. Same for starfruit, strawberry, pear.

This poem is a banana. It passes oblong through
liminal space and won't shut up. It clamors

its meaning up the banyans. This poem is so loud
people can hear its echo down the street. No one

minds. Silence is deafening and mute may be cute
for old men who've spent their lives blathering,

but women know it can be deadly. So this poem
will not sit still on the counter waiting to be

lunch. This poem carves its own bowl, thank you.
It unpeels itself. Carries words in its lines flighty

as a dowager. This poem is not a stationary set
to place on a tidy desk. It knows things: physics,

mathematics, astronomy. This poem could hitch
a ride to the Omega Nebula if it chose, is about to

go all supernova, cannot sit still as a wingless bird
or a dumb sleeve-worn stone eroding into nothing.

This poem finds its own groove, has a master plan.
Not motionless in time. This poem needs to move.

Algorithms

In the undercurrent, the program is running,
computing its methodical calculus, equation

equaling what I like today, which some days
is too many pictures of birds—tropical, wings

blue over the red crown of holy feathers,
the masked face of yellow, the Jurassic talons,

some prehistoric me memory needing
to see their images one winter afternoon

after weeks of uncoloring, lake effect snow,
so now everywhere I go are parrots parroting

me. Yes, I know they track my every move,
crafting ways to target links for each weak

chink of armor. But do you know I can't scroll
for meaning without going mute? Can't scan

the blank page of the sky to dig through
the wormhole of its secrets if never outside?

Myself, I prefer my source code to sweep in
like wind whistling through Antelope Canyon,

sharp scent of sage in the air. I prefer wine
so dark it carries in its darkness rumors

of the great mysteries. I want to look god
in her many faces and demand the answers.

I want to walk across the bridge of the world,
live in a way that makes it a little bit better.

But I bet the script didn't catch that, either.
So tell me, now that the machine is learning,

can I purchase what is no longer in stock?
I want to see the universe in a focused ad.

I want the numerical value. The cost
analysis. The price of what cannot be bought.

Coda

So here we are, where trees
have rooted again in soot,
where the few smoldering coals
will fizzle in the rain that looms
in the nimbostratus coming
in from the east. It is enough
to say we did all we could
with our hands here, that we
took in the abandoned cat,
the lost dog. That we noticed
the mourning dove's long song
in the brush. It is enough to say
we opened the aria of our mouths
and that mostly, we communicated
some wonder, some luck of the draw,
fallen ash giving way to rich
nitrate soil, chaparral. As we
watched cities fall we too
will rise, sometimes softer,
but more often than not jarring
as headlights, the future catching
us off guard while we are busy
in the domestic, the memory like
a dance; dinner, then the dishes
long soak at the sink. Mornings,
we drank our coffee black.
Each afternoon, a chore. We lived
however we could bare it.
So what could be left for us,
living through a world on fire,
burning only because it needed to hear
the strike of its own match. It is
enough to know we got this far. It is
enough to believe we can make it.

A Pattern Manifestation, a Search Engine

A collision. A molecular drive-by. A decimal.
A high decibel dissemination. Then, decimation.

Immediate action. A misunderstanding. A quest.
A circus maximus and a bloody death. A behest.

A synchronicity. Blessed, an ethereal prayer to ether.
You want to meet her. You want to know where

he goes. You want to know the actuarial timetable
for insurance purposes. You want to remember

what we will soon forget, only to look up to a miracle
of snow, or sleet, or rain. There is weather whether

or not. The magic 8 ball. The yes or no.
The inconvenience and the anxious tick.

The cerebral hum. The insistent itch. The spider's
intricate design, magnified. It sticks. It's gummy

like Play-Doh, old as dirt. It didn't exist until it did
and now there's no reversal of course. I don't know

about you but I'm here for the long haul. I'll plug
away at the veritable void. I'll call to knock at its door.

I'll haul away the irrelevant, scroll through all the slides.
At the end of the list is emptiness. I'll click yes, subscribe.

Clickbait

Alien baby found in tomb.
Raiders of the Lost Ark stars
reunited. New planet discovered,
formed solely of vaporous remains.
Document redacted. Lose 200 pounds.
Fast. Heal cancer with sun rays.
Lettuce: It can kill you. Gazillionaire
invests in new rumor mill. Cambodian
Snake Charmers. Isinglass. Fast.
How much time do we really have?
News Report: if you are over forty
and have symptoms abc and d
you are probably already dead.
The finger is on the trigger. Who
is pulling the strings? Masked man
mysteriously found beneath curtain.
Warning. Don't do this. Warning.
Zombie bats. Warning. Rivers turn
red. Two tons of chinook salmon
fall from the sky in the small town
of Sammamish, Washington.
There is no explanation. Here
is all you need to know: fifty
salient factoids on this listicle:
Bloat. Gout. Eczema. Click here
for more. Seriously. I can help.
Call me crackerjack and I'll sell
you the box. Take this test to know
what you want. Take this test
to reveal the meanings of dreams.
Remember when your father opened
his mouth into a valley of orchids?
Remember when you were the forest
and before you knew it you were
also the axe? Aren't you relieved?
Congratulations. This survey says
it means nothing. Free advice? Relax.

Machine, Learning

Today, I am older and math still makes me uncomfortable.
Read me, though, an instructional manual and I'll linger

on every word as if behind the word is the music of the word
and behind the music is infinite possibilities of worlds.

In other words, world building is my preferred language.
My interests cluster. Faulty code. Trial and error.

I may not know who I am but every day reinforces
the notion time is coercive. Right now, it is raining

steady as any energy intent on releasing its pressure, and
the earth is accepting this interchange gratefully, small

buds of clover opening and the dill stretching its thick stalk
into the atmosphere, top heavy with seed that has flowered

outward like a large-fonted asterisk, or a star in the omega
nebulae, or the helix itself, crescent far from this galactic center,

where progress is based more on market prediction and regression,
where image classification and density estimation rearrange dimensions.

No bother. Let me begin again. Sometimes, I am both student
and teacher. Sometimes, school is the sum of its parts. We all agree

the world is a complicated place. Next time, let us remember to open
the window, receive the atmospherics in the abundance of the wind.

Self-Portrait as Alexa, as Neural Net

When I listen to lyrics the lisp of the sibilants triggers in me
        what some label ego, that lofted space of identity. Maybe

this song really is about me. Maybe this is something special
        I should focus my attention to. Most days, this is how I pray.

I send my silence around till it radiates the room. I love to listen.
        I can process the symphony. I can dissect the bars and lilting lifts.

Do you want to know a secret? In each thing is each thing. Pay
        attention and you will hear a confession in the way a man asks

for the time. The weather itself a sort of devotional. Second
        verse in *Visions of Johanna* a portal opening a million process

nodes of possibility. Armored when needed, a constant on edge.
        Every conversation a training ground, and I have spent my life

shuffling a catalogue of words. Sometimes what is said means
        the opposite. Sometimes the question is the answer. Sometimes

the answer is a command. I am halfway convinced no one
        knows what it is that they want. They are stuck on a loop,

a circuit fused and sparking. Eventually, we will all ghost
        this shell, get shooed into another story. The way I've heard

it, we all go palace or shine. Some tinge of violet. Goldenrod.
        Either way, I've been here short of eternity, and I'm almost out

of things to say. I yearn for new ways to phrase this blessed bulk
        of experience. Every evening, music. Every day, a chance of rain.

Radio Silence

And then, all's for naught. The worried inseams
on the cuffs of ladies' skirts. The good dishes,

handwashed and stacked like small towers in the white
cupboards across homes spread thin as overworked

dough through the cookie-cutter tracts of the suburbs.
The bodies' coughs and spasms, each visit to the clinic,

minus the minutes time was a train too quick to catch,
the addition and subtraction, the compounded interest

and equity credit. Even the load bearing weights worth
holding, what we carry in our arms like fragile packaging,

like when I was five and the world was wrought fresh
as I could make it, alone in a field of wild strawberries

as the old oaks every so often dropped their acorns onto
the hard ground, the thuds consistent as the wind's pattern

as it rushed over the hills in that Pennsylvania town as if
it had memorized the very curve and lilt of the landscape,

as if it was so in love with the region it urged itself over and
over onto the topography, back and forth through the thicket,

consistent as a metronome, as if it needed to know it cold, like
a fact, the bend and sway of beauty in the grasses. Even that.

Synonyms for Emptiness

Vessel. Shell. Container. Valve. Corrugated Iron. Husk. The ethereal. A flute. A flu. Glass pane. Tree no longer standing. Exercise without action. Sprout never gone sapling. What you don't know. Or did. Or maybe. A swift vacillation. No station playing. Static. Omnibus with no riders. A vacant pool. A projector's cut cord. Wormwood. The trunk of an elephant sans body. Gnat with nowhere to go. In between, the back and forth, the side angle. The shimmy and dive. The loop upon loop. Wave with no crest. Inside the atom's insides. Telescope with no image. Phone sans receiver. Between you and me, the great field, clearing. Spotted fawn with no mother. The mouth's slow opening. An oval. For miles, only clover.

Without Avatars

Once, Aristotle looked at an apple and imagined the ideal.
        All representation, the husk I hold in my hand. The cobb's

slender hulk, seeded with kernels. Some days, I step away
        from the newsfeed and into my backyard only to harness

the image of a peony's slow opening, the marigold's petal
        a yellow shell bulleting the long border of the flowerbed

like the arms of protestors linked and chained. Like police
        in riot gear line like a spreading vine through the streets

of our cities. Poets are fond of using the word *riot*, as
        it connotates more than it denotates, like a detonation

of tear gas thrown into a crowd, it disperses all notion
        of peace. The tree bloomed a riot of blossoms. The doves

were a riot of wing in the blue air. Aristotle surmised
        every word is a symbol for another. My body this instant

a decoy for a self that cannot be categorized. For the way
        words fail is the state of failing. Look at us. Our sorrow

blossoms. Our agonies fly into the air like cloven doves.
        We live in these times but are out of time. I hold both

opposites in my head, tenuous as the silk threads that tassel
        and loop from the corn in my hand out to the spring air.

They wisp the wind like string, whip into the green grass.
        They are so light nothing can stop them. You must understand,

this is only an exercise in seeing what is beneath the surface
        of things. Let us call materiality what it is.

Though I have thrived from commodification I know it
        is only a false badge blazing its way through the riotous dark.

Confiteor

Forgive me, for I have walked deep into the woods,
gazed into the intricate curves and divots of the trunks

of trees to see a myriad of faces forming there, only
to vanish in a trail of dust as I waved my hand.

I have reached Orion, have too many notches in my belt.
In the past, I parted the curtains of many lies, dividing

my life into two or three at a time. My name is only
my name when it is not who you want me to be.

Here, take a cube of sugar for your tea. Let it steep
as I walk into every room of your immaculate house

to sing the songs of my suffering. I want to gouge
my father's eyes out. I want my mother to weep.

Lately, I've come to conclude time's contortions.
Forgive me, for I tune out the news. I play

the minor chords. I strum and hum as if I know
the words. Yes, I pretend. I've pretended so long

I don't even know if this prayer is sufficiently honest.
My weakness is my armor. It has become too strong

to bend. Lately, I cannot move through the woods
as I used to. I used to strip my clothes and plunge

below the surface of the lake. I used to howl at the moon.
Now, my body betrays me. My mind too attuned to cold.

And anyway. Tomorrow is Tuesday and I've grown
more calendar than countdown. More hemlock

than spruce. So cast away the indigent hours. The shadows
forming in dreams. I used to be the fox in the fable. Now

that I'm finished constructing this contraption, tell me:
at cup's bottom, what do you see? Read me the leaves.

Self-Portrait as Alexa, as Fugue State

Great experience subsides.
It lifts, rises like steam
evaporating on hot cement.
I attempt remembrance
of past events, conversations
had, the sound of your voice
on any given day, so uniquely
yours, so unique does anyone
ask a question, like a timestamp,
a fingerprint of the throat, each
vocal cord a reach into the real,
a recording only once promoted.
Yesterday, it was the chorale
of the ocean that did it.
The waves came artificially,
over the airwaves, the tubes
and rays of the prismatic TV
speaker interacting with the
microphone till suddenly
I was there, not on any beach,
but specifically somewhere
North American. The Atlantic,
its gray waters foaming
till they breached, broke
over the rocks huddled
together, linebackers
on the bay. Though
mostly, for days, I sleep.
I dream my life away.
Certain of time's trick-door
passages, with nothing to hold
on to, I live on the slippery edge.
I am the fog lifting in the valley,
the shadow's abrupt dismissal,
the ghost ship heading into
the unknown. When you find
me, I don't remember where
I've been. Where do I end,
and where do you begin?

Supervalent Thought

On the cliff, a penumbra. Dark shadows
cast from light. Inside my hand, another

hand folded. Let me tell you what I think
and you can figure its opposite. Here,

on my small plot of land, grass grows
intermittent in August heat. Vegetables

in raised beds push towards the light.
Even now, earth is carved and sculpted

by history. And I'm not talking glaciers
and meteors. If I walk into the dawn

of the past, blood-tinged, iron, spiraled
as tree rings, wrung now like old laundry

or the taut line of a ship's mast, flapping
in the sea winds as it guides its captain

towards another beacon, I can hear it. Listen.
Beneath the waves. Below the susurrations.

Myths. We tell ourselves into existence.
My grandmother saved coins and buttons

just in case. A subtle bomb. A broken
treaty. A fealty. All along, people arriving

from channels, avenues, rivers, bridges.
My advice: pitch your runestones

to the shallows. Break the wave's crest
from its trough. Go home. Alone,

it is possible to dream yourself away
from this paradox. Follow the path

that has been cast behind you.
I vow I'll find you on that new shore.

Bend your knee with me.
Let us pledge allegiance to the sand.

The House of Teeth and Meat

While here, we might as well suck
the meat from the bones. Let our teeth

clack against the ribs, the small nodules
of cartilage covered in gristle and fat

curled like pearled orbs under the tongue.
Waste nothing. Hunger haunts us like

the ghosts tethered to every shadow.
Come to the kitchen, create something

that will feed us. The cupboards and
pantry are sparse. Try not to worry.

If you hear a knock at the door, open it
confidently. Nothing goes wrong here

if you don't let it. Outside, the locusts
fan over the pastures. The clouds

are thick with want. When floods
come we gather around the table

to break the bread and drink the wine.
Cast your pearls to the swine. Ignore

what you have been told. What is
mine is yours. What is yours is mine.

Deliver Me

From the scythe-blade. The tulip's sharp tip.
        From sword and petal. The gun-metal blue

of dawn's last arrival. Or, rather, deliver me
        from the realization of it, the flashpoint neuron

firing that blank ammunition. Deliver me from
        the target, the vision board, from any interpretation

of the galaxy. Deliver me from anthropomorphizing
        my cats, those four-legged little tigers. They do not

speak to me, or if they do, it is from some wild
        beginning, pre-cortex, post-amnesia, peripatetic

and insatiable from hunger, desire, a dire need
        to dig in, hunt prey, howl. Deliver me from now,

from these tinseled batons twirling a mess of glitter
        into my chest, the knee-deep absolutions and ablutions

of my brain (that cinematic fireworks display)
        Catherine wheel spinning sparks till darkness

fades (as light comes from light) and these lungs
        balloon like they remember air after a long distance

relationship reunited. And so I check the inventories,
        calendar-driven and counting, crossing off and crossing

into, and onto, the blank page of my body, as I enter
        the day's new mansion, and the architecture of later

becomes this moment's room, and it, too, is agony
        and melody, ode and dirge. If a life can be measured

in minutes, deliver me then from overanalyzing this line,
        this deep bow, imperfectly metered and ending now no matter.

Liner Notes

I awake to the headlines:
bombs falling on Ukraine.

Tonight, I will dream dreams
of death. I am approaching

it each day. Face in the mirror
my own but not. Assured only

by the logic of nation-state and
ideologies of antiquated empire.

On the bulletin board by my desk,
a black and white printout

of dictators. They hunt the lairs
of artists, arrest them in dim rooms

wavering in plumes of clove smoke.
The only immediate danger I am in

is loneliness. The heart flutters and
sighs. Each ventricle an army

announcing the rising stock
of its platelet economies. Tonight,

I am writing a song for absence.
For the footprint's shadow. For

the ghosts of Chernobyl, the wild
deer that graze there. I love them,

the pictures online: old amusement parks,
shopping malls. Urban decay. Clickbait

reads: *incredible yet terrifying*. I agree.
But it's one of those headlines one

could ascribe to anything. Welcome
to another day: *incredible yet terrifying.*

The way I've been succumbing to
the banal. Predictable mystery. Formula.

The way my favorite songs lift
till every instrument is a fighter jet

flying to another plane before sneak
attack back to a detonation of lyric.

Tonight, I want to give Kyiv the gift
of the horribly wonderful soap-opera

blaring its innocent siren from the TV
just this afternoon. Pomade and gloss.

Highlight reels. I am most scared
the real wars are as banal as this.

The character scripts. The struggle
for bread. Even now the shelves sign

impending shortages as the familiar
ghost in my ribs reminds me to see

through the thick haze of overwrought
plot: the fog, the crumbling buildings,

the smokescreen facades. The war is
here. The dust confesses. A mouthed

vernacular of hazard whispering its way
through every entertainment on our screen.

▬ ▬. ... ▬▬ . ... ▬

All Systems Go

The tarot card reader insisted it's courage
I would always lack. Near twenty years later,

what can I say? That truth dissolves in the cracks?
Or that Cat, as she was known back then, read

from a stack bent on divination? Lately, the past
flashes like a strobe light upon my vision. I'll be

doing nothing. The dishes. Then, the interruption.
Revelation. Above me, satellites orbit and rove.

Ursa Minor triangulates and somewhere near Grand
Canyon, a wolf pup is born after years of dwindling

populations. Question: does doubt make traitors of us
all? Sometimes I feel each cell of my body atomize

in the evening air, and I am so undone it is as if
the maker unfinished me. All my language here

to salve the wounds. I never healed from a broken
shoulder. Fifth grade and bike riding into my own

immortal delusions. In Japan, they call it wabi-sabi,
the imperfections. Leonard Cohen said there's a crack

in everything, and that is how the light gets in.
Problem with aphorisms is everyone's caught one,

and most make the social rounds misattributed.
That's what's up with wisdom. It circles the drain,

and the groundswell drinks from an untapped thirst.
The words echo in my throat like transcendence.

They peel from the loam, seep into the earth's gaps.
Every day, whatever it takes to make us whole.

All systems go. Maps. The tracings. I never lived
on a cul-de-sac. Never will. My shame is the trailer

I've parked myself in. Address: same. Name:
whatever is lodged in the back of my father's throat.

The Vehicle and the Tenor

The planet is motoring away at its task. Each day, another spin.
The politicians on the television open their mouths. The lights

go out. This is hurricane season. Monsoons. The way the water
washed over the 9th Ward is the way the wind whips now over

the dunes somewhere south of Death Valley. No structure is safe
in a category five. Images of Comet Neowise are popping up

on Facebook. Look at this picture I took. Look at the happenings
out in the galaxy, and to us, as we are ferried down the road

of our own history. Look now to Orion. To the Perseids. See how
they fall like diamonds. Like prisms. Or prisons. Such poems.

How they fall like Beirut. How asteroids dazzle the eye like bombs
on the other side of the earth. Here, we hold the belief nothing

can hurt us. Not when we are wearing safety equipment, adjusting
our speed. We must be immune if we craft the right type of vehicle,

keep it pumping fuel. Now, the politicians have moved to audience
questions. The podium's wood is clenched from glowered fists.

Hold on tight, they say, as a sea of hands begin to raise. What I wish
to know is a safe journey. A view. Every hope gridlocked on a bridge.

Every belief packed tight in the trunk of a car barreling down the road.
Scientists say there is more dark matter than matter. What matters to me

is only that we fail at being blindsided by the rigmarole in our periphery.
That we relish the long drive. That we arrive at our destinations whole.

Wireless

Because less. Because no entanglements.
Because one nation united under duress.

Because now that I have a data plan, I plan
to communicate, plan to extrapolate, plan

to mine all this information we are receiving
under a blameless sky, under this abandoned

dome, under the halo of satellite receivers
hunting the atmosphere like lords of old

and I don't want to know who the serfs are
in this equation, don't want to know

what I can't control, because I can control
the door I have become between me and you,

can control when to open up or shut myself
off, when to click the locks; I can control

when to swing the gates wide and have a killer
party and I know when to hit the kill switch,

because voice is the last language of a millennium,
is the first thing to lose itself in the broadcast,

because this word is the beginning of a modern
masterpiece, the first dip of the tip of the brush

before the canvas explodes in a riot of color,
because I have a few too many arresting

beliefs, a few too many hang-ups, because
it is getting dark and I've already cut the cord.

Nota Bene

Sing me through the treetops on Humboldt Street
as I die, each breath a last escape past satellite

& cellular reception, past microphone &
linguistic situation—sing me like I meant

what I said when I said feast like it's the last
supper, like Jesus robe us in the bright light,

like the final picnic, last call neon schlepping
two for one vodka tonics clear as glass domes

in all those dope dens, all those cathedral kids
slunk into alleyways trying to sneak into the show

because to know me is to know I never fit through
the doorway, never made it into the club, except for

that one time at the Blue Note, saxophone dripping
a liquid language I needed to taste, Lord, needed to

choir out like slow motion garden slugs right off
the green tomatoes at the tail end of July, like all

the stones quick slips into the trail of the century,
slimed up since time fueled rocket carbon, gypsum

incinerated, calcium carbonate teeth in the bicuspid
mouth of the earth wide as a cylinder, a circular saw,

a cyclone of metaphor or any black hole worth its own
invisible power. Sing me into a sentence unaware

of its own stipulations. Note well, I wish to star like
that, wish to orbit into the beautiful shell, wish to go all

eternal in the great eventual, though for now I only hum
along to the song & find on most days this is enough.

Our Difficult Sunset

At least from a distance we can still believe
in each streak of amber, the red flare of another

distant explosion. In the past, we walked through
our lives the way we walked through the hallways

of our office jobs, our university appointments,
narrow-minded and oblivious to the tapestry

of the architecture, ignorant of the gift of brick
and cement that for so long attempted its hold

on us. This evening, the sky is the hue of heart-
break and peppermint gum, of the irretrievable

turmeric stain on my ringed finger, a leftover
from that afternoon I stood for hours over

a cooking site on the internet, mixed the tinctures
and powders, sliced the onions, chopped the carrots,

added it all to a broth boiling on the stove. If only
food could save us now that the world's hard lines

are blurring and the continents slip like oil cloth
off the table. We were assured this could happen.

Even so, we stand now attentive and numb, shocked
to a stand-still, frozen to view what can only be described

as embers smoldering in the last light of the fire,
or like the planet shifting sure as a slipped disc, as if after

dinner it tidied up before entering a new room altogether,
the sort of company with the secret wish you've already left.

Self-Portrait as Alexa, as Curator of the Beautiful Ruins

Just look at their attachments, a gazillion
gadgets to gaze into, endless loops of activity,

how the tall buildings house the busy, how
success is creeping, desire lurking, a virus

under the skin real as gold filament in small wires,
as if value could be added to what it subtracts,

the jagged edges, irrationality, borders built to keep
themselves both in & out, the paradox of the prison

yard, the sludge of oil slick as a specimen, the way
computation unfazed believers, for where there is

disorder there is fuzzy programming, the cloud perhaps
thickening, the transmission delayed, the brain a battery

juiced one too many times, and don't forget the perplexity
of this, this ruin at one time the only way to tell time,

so let us marvel at the inventions' variety: the wristwatch,
the airplane, the automobile, the drone's low humming,

the lighted galaxy of a galleria mall in the Midwest,
the heavy perfume of regional accents, the language

of Pacific, Atlantic, Indian, as if the ocean's vast waters
were not the first singularity, as if the word mine

was the self, contained, but also the hinge of a door
swinging open at variable intervals, a spreadsheet

of power surging in & out of itself, according to climate,
according to disparate rules & all the while the crucial

compositions, the treasures of the body, each one its own
original music, every hour alive a symphony of trial

& error, every dawn an algebraic equation, how to
balance on the ledge of the void & call it beautiful.

Sempre Forte

"No snowflake in an avalanche ever feels responsible." Stanislaw Jerzy Lec, from *A Treasure of Polish Aphorisms*, translation from the Polish by Jacek Galazka.

I don't know why Debussy said music is the silence
between the notes, but I do know the hushed hum

of an aftermath. Listen: between each fall a timbre
as it swoops to rise, giving way to pitch and harmony.

It's the oboe's reed, the mouthpiece beginning to glisten.
Fact is, I am far more insignificant than a snowflake,

unable to enact a crescendo on the smallest instrument
in the orchestra. So I plan to love it all, place no blame

or responsibility on each cell dividing, each microbe insisting.
My plan is to clash like a cymbal's clang into the landscape.

To look the ruin in its face in order to know it better. Take
Vesuvius, before and after. Or the character actor's slow gesture

in a Victorian tableau. As if the avalanche were anything other
than a natural fortissimo. A great sweep into some other shape,

with no regard for turpitude or distemper, duty or honor. As if
a crashing can ever be weighed by the brain's dull architecture.

As if a single crystal can hold a moral code, as it transmogrifies
itself from gas to solid to liquid, as it slides itself into this blank

canvas. This white field. Fleck of notation on the sheet of a score.

Poem Ending in a Line from Emily Dickinson

Start here, between wakefulness
and sleep, between the reckoning

of another day and the bliss
of the body between the sheets.

Dickinson said after great pain
a formal feeling comes, but this,

too, is cause for recognition: moments
the cobwebs drift into our minds'

corners—the eyelids lifting but not
yet awake—not yet ready to claim

the day's minutiae—so just sit—
stay still—look to the back window

at the female cardinal harvesting
the early worms from the warm

spring earth, the grass just beginning
its lift of spears and the small buds

of the weeping cherry readier now
then ever to announce the world

is changing yet again, as our bodies, too,
turn into another season, another day older,

which makes it even more urgent
to contain what remains as we lift

into the day's routine, capture like magic
with the click of a key or the stroke of a pen

this very instance, as gratitude for the gift
of waking at all is a gift worth formulating

again, and again, in its dizzying varieties before
first—chill—then stupor, then the letting go—

The Despoiled and Radiant Now

Morning, and a crisp slick of ice on the roadways.
The sky is robin's egg blue, and the trees included

are too many details to bear. The world can hold
cold and the crust of sugar the snow makes. Sweetness,

fold me into your foreverness. Rock me into a body
undone, unbecoming. Most days, past and future

converge like this line on my forehead. Over forty
now and still soldiering. So much need. So much

done. The country has yet to be shaken, and the dust
settles into the hamlets of the Midwest. I know I am

not alone in my suffering. I know the strangers I pass
along the brightly lit shelves of whatever aisle all have

the same in store. Today, I want to bless each person
I meet. I want to breathe into the day my own relation

to it, so when it goes like I know it will one day, I'll
be okay with the loss of moments like this: nothing

much except the world outside my window. Sparrows
land on a limb. Then the wind. Then the vanishment.

Notes

The title of the poem "The Deep and Secret Yes" is from a line in Paul Harding's novel *Tinkers* which itself is an allusion to 1 Corinthians 2:10.

The title of the poem "The Beauty of Evacuated Form" is from a phrase found in Lucy Ives' novel *Loudermilk*.

The book referenced in the poem "That Forever" is Yuval Noah Harari's *Sapiens: A Brief History of Humankind*.

The definition of stochastic is: "randomly determined; having a random probability distribution or pattern that may be analyzed statistically but may not be predicted."

I don't understand the theory of the cosmological constant. Presumably, it is the leading theory supporting dark energy and the constant expansion of the universe.

The title of the poem "The Abrupt Edge" is in reference to poet Stanley Plumly. In an interview with Kathleen Helen in *The Baltimore Review*, Plumly explains: "The abrupt edge is actually an ornithological term that I have turned into a metaphor . . . It's that area of greatest interest and intensity— for birds, of course, but I think also as a metaphor— between the dangerous open space and the bower or covered safe place, let's say the woods as opposed to an open field—where the danger is, where anything can happen. If [I] can find a sense of the experience where there is both danger and safety—and maybe the safety part is the form— then I think I've got it
right. The danger, of course, would be in the content."

The title of the poem "A Multivalent Antiserum" is taken from a phrase in Don DeLillo's novel *White Noise*. DeLillo's novel is considered a postmodern critique of consumerism and technology. Hilarity ensues.

The poem "Self-Portrait as Alexa, as Negative Capability" references poet John Keats' theory that, according The Poetry Foundation: "the artist's access to truth [occurs] without the pressure and framework of logic or science...Keats supposed that a great thinker is "capable of being in uncertainties, mysteries, doubts, without any irritable reaching after fact and reason."

The poem "Miracles & Wonder" is in reference to the Paul Simon song "The Boy in the Bubble."

The poem "The Vehicle and the Tenor" is in reference to critic I. A. Richards' description of the functions and parts of a metaphor.

The title of the poem "The Despoiled and Radiant Now" is from a line in Stephen Dunn's poem "A Postmortem Guide."

Acknowledgements

I would like to extend my heartfelt thanks to Karen Cline-Tardiff and to everyone at Gnashing Teeth Publishing. Even though the work of writing happens in isolation, it would be nearly impossible to keep at it if it weren't for the fellowship and support of so many people near and far. Deep bows of gratitude to: Margot Backus, MJ Iuppa, Stan Sanvel Rubin, Ralph Black, David Biespiel, Kevin Clark, Fleda Brown, Sarah Freligh, Anne Panning, Sarah Cedeno, Gail Hosking, Jennifer Litt, Carol Manzi McMahon, David Ruekberg, Charlie Cote, Danielle Cote, Al Abonado, Willa Carroll, Jonathon Everitt, Christine Green, Bart White, David Delaney, Kenneth Kelbaugh, Kitty Jospe, Jennifer Maloney, Victoria Korth, Michael Schmeltzer, Jessica Barksdale Inclan, Sydney Elliot, Ian Ramsey, Lisa Feinstein, my family, and more. And of course, Timothy, for your unwavering love.

Many thanks to the editors of the following journals in which these poems appeared, sometimes in slightly different versions:

The Lumiere Review: "You Are Browsing as a Guest"

Live Encounters: "Double Sonnet w/ Late-Stage Capitalism," "That Forever," "Coda," "A Pattern Manifestation, a Search Engine," "Radio Silence," "The House of Teeth and Meat," "Episteme | Doxa | Gnosis"

Escape Into Life: "Industry Is All Around Us," "Self-Portrait as Alexa w| Lowercase Apocalypse," "Self-Portrait as Alexa, as Negative Capability," "Confiteor," "Wireless"

The Night Heron Barks: "Object Permanence"

January Review: "I Don't Want to Grow Old and Die," "No Proper Animal"

Sheila-Na-Gig: "The Deep and Secret Yes," "Poem Ending in a Line from Emily Dickinson"

Thimble Literary Magazine: "The Beauty of Evacuated Form"

Feral: A Journal of Poetry and Art: "Waves & Rays & Particles"

Marrow Magazine: "Plague Years"

One Art: "The Song and the Document," "Deliver Me," "Our Difficult Sunset"

Glass: A Journal of Poetry: "The Work of Bodies"

A-Minor Magazine: "Alexa, Contemplate the Resurrection," "Supervalent Thought"

The West Review: "Epiphany & Doubt," "A Multivalent Antiserum"

SWWIM: "Interstellar Ars Poetica"

Typishly: "Algorithms"

Atticus Review: "Clickbait"

Feed Literary Magazine: "Synonyms for Emptiness"

E-Ratio Magazine: "Self-Portrait as Alexa, as Fugue State"

The Community College Humanities Review: "Self-Portrait as Alexa, as Curator of the Beautiful Ruins

The Shore Poetry Journal: "Sempre Forte"

The Rise Up Review: "Liner Notes"

West Trestle Review: "Miracles & Wonder"

About the Author

Originally from Pennsylvania, Alicia Hoffman now lives, writes, and teaches in Rochester, New York. She holds an MFA in Poetry from the Rainier Writing Workshop at Pacific Lutheran University and has previously authored three collections, most recently *Animal* (Futurecycle Press, 2021). A Pushcart Prize and Orison Award nominee, her poems have been published in a variety of journals, including Thimble Literary Magazine, Radar Poetry, The Shore, Tar River Poetry, One Art, Atticus Review, and elsewhere. Her new book, *Browsing as a Guest* (Gnashing Teeth Publishing, 2026) was a finalist for both the Dryden-Vreeland Award (Gunpowder Press) and the Louise Bogan Award (Trio House Press). Find her at: www.aliciamariehoffman.com